I'M YOUR
PUSHER

TANISHA O. HAMILTON

All Scripture quotations, unless otherwise indicated, are taken from The Holy Bible, New International Version® NIV®. Copyright © 1973, 1978, 1984, 2011 by Biblica, Inc.™

Verses marked NKJV are taken from the New King James Version of The Bible.

Verses marked KJV are taken from the King James Version of The Bible.

Cover photo by Rodgers Polk Photography

Copyright © 2020 by Tanisha O. Hamilton

All rights reserved. No part of this publication may be reproduced, stored in any form of retrieval system or transmitted in any form or by any means without prior permission in writing from the publishers except for the use of brief quotations in a book review.

Published by Write-On Publishing. This book and all other Write-On Publishing books are available online, at bookstores and distributors worldwide.

Contact: tanishaohamilton.com

Dedication

To God for empowering and entrusting me with this ink that will never run dry as it will serve as a catalyst to push everyone to strategically and boldly lay hold of everything He has for them.

To my faithful and supportive children who have shown me unconditional love throughout this journey.

To my parents, family members, friends, prayer warriors and colleagues who encouraged me through prayer, texts, and phone calls.

To everyone who allows me to be YOUR PUSHER!

STRATEGIC EXECUTION DETAILS

Unfolding History 5

Chapter 1 Taking Zero Steps 11

Chapter 2 Not Without My Children 13

Chapter 3 We're Better Together 29

Chapter 4 I've Got You Covered 31

Chapter 5 Blur 33

Chapter 6 Walk It Out 49

Chapter 7 Diabolical Schedule 53

Chapter 8 Double Weekends 57

Chapter 9 Cut the Umbilical Cord 77

Chapter 10 The 3 Y's Men 83

UNFOLDING HISTORY

*When opportunity knocks, you answer, and then
jam your foot in the door.*

Where It All Began

I did not always want to be a nurse. I knew I wanted to be an integral part of the medical field as in high school I was in an engineering dual-enrollment magnet program. My first career choice, so I thought anyway, was going to be a biomedical engineer which was the happy middle of being in the medical field, changing lives, and not having to deal with blood. While I was in high school and continued to my freshman year of college, I worked in the pharmacy at a large retail pharmacy chain. After being exposed to that, I thought here is another option to become a Pharmacist. They worked long hours, looked like they enjoyed themselves, and were providing, in some cases, life-sustaining medications. So I went off to college in pursuit of becoming a research pharmacist. Why a research pharmacist and not retail? I knew I did not want to deal with direct customers asking me to supply them with small doses of their medications until their insurance company authorized it.

    I envisioned myself wearing a long white lab coat, walking up to the door, and putting my hands on the screen to open it, entering to conduct research then in about six months or so sending down some new drug to the consumers. The faces of the elderly, the desperate pleas of parents who needed medications for their children, or themselves; it made me nauseous every time I thought about going to work. So I quickly ended the retail pharmacy position I had for a short stint in college. I wanted a career where I could help more people solve their problems. That brings me to my voracious pursuit of the most anointed career on the planet, nursing.

    Nursing is truly a calling. In my opinion, it is the only career that you can do anywhere in the world. Take this visual journey with me. An individual can be a nurse on the land, this includes acute care hospital settings, rehab, grocery stores, schools, gyms, basically any industry, in the air, yes airlines, private jets, under the water, on a cruise ship, and even on an island. You can even go international if that doesn't scream choose me as a passionate pursuit of helping and satisfaction, I don't know what does.

Go for it, you have nothing to lose.

I was previously admitted into a nursing program in August 2009, but I was unsuccessful in a class not related to the material. It was a clinical check-off course, but with the way they allocated points and how the classes were grouped into theoretical and clinical I was unable to continue my studies. That seemingly ended my nursing education. I was devastated. The reality of what had happened brought on an onslaught of feelings of defeat and turmoil. Here is the actual information from my acceptance letter so you can grasp the magnitude of this. There were 748 applicants competing for 325 seats in the August 2009 nursing class. 325 candidates were selected who earned between 8 - 22 total points. Alternates are selected to fill any seats that become available however, this number accounts for 10% of the seats being offered, in this class there would be 30 alternates. If I wanted to continue at this school, I was going to have to sit out for an unknown number of semesters before the class rotation came around. I allowed myself to have that pow–wow moment for about 2 to 3 days. My classmates were distraught and maintained their encouragement but at the time I was over that and had started looking for an alternative route. There was no way that one school was going to be the end of me and my dreams. So I called, visited, and researched nursing school programs throughout the State of Florida. I was willing to relocate to any part of the state. What I found was exorbitant amounts of time on the waiting lists and waiting for two-three years or unknown was not an option for me. It couldn't be. Time was of the essence, my children were younger and the lifestyle options I had envisioned for them was going to happen, period.

I called my best friend from high school and began to pour out my utter frustration and determination to him and his wife. I called them daily, each time I acquired new nursing school information throwing question after question, and thought after thought their way. Hey, what do you think? This one seems too long. What about this one? He often called to make sure I was doing okay. Not only was he my best friend but he and his wife knew the field. They were both military nurses, who resided in Texas. It is always great to have a listening ear and a nonjudgmental voice available for support when you feel as though your dreams may have slipped through your fingers as easily as a raindrop. They encouraged me to pursue my goals in a different location, Texas being one they could speak from experience about. They both agreed I could do it and that it really did not make sense to wait.

I prayed and pondered all the possible choices. My number one concern was my two precious children, their safety was paramount, their educational pathway was vital and their transitions to another state needed to be easy. How would this affect their relationships with our family and other little cousins?

The same assured statement, "you have nothing to lose and everything to gain" always came to mind. That right there is a loaded statement, one of trust. I had trusted God before and knew Him to be faithful. One of promise, that I was going to gain something better, and one of endearment, really, I knew the results of where I was already. I am not a "what if" person, "maybe I should do this" type of person. I decide and follow through because by the time I make a decisive action I have already sought advice from a multitude of credible sources.

In order to finish a thing, you have to start that thing.

What a great day to share my decision. I wasn't even going to stop by this house. After driving all day from Palm Beach to Miami visiting and dining with family and friends, the last thing on my mind was to make another stop at a celebration for my mom's friend. There comes a time in everyone's life where you must decide to do better. That moment of a catapult decision arrived in November as I was at a friend's Thanksgiving celebration in Florida. Stomach happy, tired and thinking about the long ride home, I decided I had been there way too long and was leaving to go home. When I got outside, I didn't even realize he was sitting outside and had literally walked right by him. He asked why I was leaving so early, I said "Early for you but today is far spent plus I need to start packing for my move." "Move! To where?" Nonchalantly, I informed him that I was leaving Florida and moving to Texas to pursue my nursing degree. As you can imagine there was the initial shock of someone really leaving Florida to go to Texas. The common statements, well what is in Texas, besides horses and cowboys. That conversation lasted about three hours until my mom was leaving, and she said I thought you left a long time ago. I said that was the plan until I got interrogated outside. I assured him, there was so much more for me and my children and I was going to find out. I had exhausted waiting for Florida and their three years to indefinite waiting list. My goals and desires were driving me forward and I had the support of my parents, friends, and peace within myself that the decision was well thought out from a multitude of counselors. I was very thankful to have their support for my decision.

CHAPTER 1
TAKING ZERO STEPS

In my first attempt to grab hold of my dreams, I was admitted into two different programs with a January 2011 start date. I decided to allow my son and daughter to remain with my family to maintain stability. My family was going to transport my children to school and extracurricular activities, a driver that could assist my family if needed was hired. I called daily to check on them. I spoke with the school Administrator and the front desk receptionist because they saw them daily. A few times I was able to speak with the classroom assistant because she was relieving the teachers and answered the phones. I also had a long family history with my son's barber. He and my best friend were friends from barber school, he also previously trimmed my brother's hair and was also the first person to cut my son's hair.

I'M YOUR PUSHER

This was the first time I had ever been without my kids. I missed their physical presence so much. I was not gone for a long period of time, it was a short calendar three-months but I missed the smiles, hugs, kisses, laughter, and just hanging out together. I had decided that I was going to visit them for spring break but the moments leading to that seemed like they were dragging by slowly. Once I spoke with my son's barber, I knew I needed to return instead of a brief visit. He said your son misses you. He looks like he lost his ace bouquet. That statement cut to the core and I needed to regroup the crew. Of course, I was overjoyed about the current opportunity but saddened about what my son was going through. I was not willing to sacrifice his happiness. After all, I was doing this for us. We enjoy and appreciate being around each other.

CHAPTER 2
NOT WITHOUT MY CHILDREN

I shared my decision to return to Florida with my best friend who had originally encouraged me to venture to Texas. I let him know that auto transportation would get in touch with him for my vehicle. As far as my other items, just storing them out of his way was sufficient with me. I traveled to visit my children as planned which was a surprise to them, then I informed them that we would be leaving as a family to go to Texas the next time around. This time I refused to pursue my dream without my children. We would do this together or not at all.

Joyful is the person who finds wisdom, the one who gains understanding.

—*Proverbs 3:13 NLT*

Four months had elapsed but the fervor and desire to provide a better opportunity intensified. I was miserable at home. Let me add a clarifying thought here, I had my children present with me and we were surrounded by people who cared. My children were being provided for and I was gainfully employed. However, I desired to be the provider for my family in every way and I was unable to do that being back at home. That made my present situation miserable to me. What else could a person want? I wanted more. Once again, I heard you have nothing to lose but everything to gain. I wanted more than the dreams, visions, and aspirations of being a nurse, but I wanted to accomplish my goal of becoming a nurse. My thoughts became bombarded with this dream. I am not even sure how I came across the nursing school that I applied for but if I had to take a guess, I probably heard of it from my friend and his wife as they were telling me about different schools. I applied to the registered nursing program at a particular school, but here is the thing, they didn't have an open spot. The counselor called to inform me that while they didn't have an open slot for the registered nursing program, I already had the admissions requirements for the licensed vocational program. I was not sure what type of nurse that was.

Once he educated me, it was simply a difference of terminology between your geographical location. LVN (Licensed Vocational Nurse), LPN (Licensed Practical Nurse). They have the same function and educational requirements. He wanted to know if I wanted to be submitted for that program and then put on the waitlist for the other program. The waitlist decision had intense timing in that they do not provide notifications until after the first day of the program. I was going to have to make a quick decision. I mean you do not wake up in Florida on Monday and relocate your family on the same day with an expectation of attending class on that day. This would be absurd and irresponsible, to say the least. It was time for a definitive action plan because this time my children would not be left behind. We were going forward together no matter what. I emphatically told the counselor yes, submit me.

Have you ever said something out of your mouth, and it wasn't until your ears heard it you realized the statement you made? That was me at that moment. I was hopeful, excited, and committed. I realized how bold and determined I was. I was never scared of relocating to another state in which we did not know anyone. Let me pose the question that many of you may be wondering about. Tanisha, do you feel as though this was a good decision because it was a step in the right direction? I knew this was unequivocally a good decision that was going to be pivotal not only in my life, but my children and everyone attached to me. While I had that tenacious grit in the fiber of my being, well-meaning people including my mother asked me if I was scared, going to a place where we did not know anyone. I repeatedly told them; "I know God and He is with us."

The intensity and hunger burned within me day and night. It continued to progress over the weeks and a few months. Yes, the plan of action was achieved, I had researched on the internet basic relocation things to be aware of. I also ordered the free relocation to the city that can be obtained from the Visitors Bureau. Now off to get the players for team success with my children which included childcare, excellent school district, barbershop and beautician, and entertainment.

> *Nothing will work unless you do.*
> *—Maya Angelou*

As I made a list of relocation things to consider, it became apparent that I had received the confirmation from God to go forward. The first time I went to Texas I met a young lady who was also a single parent, working nights, and aspiring to complete her education. We hit it off immediately because we had a lot in common, basically too much to do with the same amount of time to get it done and no room for error. I do not remember if she had called to check on me or vice versa, nonetheless I made her aware of my intention to return to Texas and that I was going to need employment. Would you be surprised if I told you that she had information about an employment position that was posted? The post was not written in fancy, eloquent speech or on a quality stock of paper from what I could gather. The font was excessively small and did not list benefits, but what it did have was a solicitation for immediate start. Neon signs, trumpets blowing, this was definitely a divine sign I was not going to pretend to not see or want.

I inquired about the post. There was such a nice and pleasant voice on the other end. She provided me with the application via email and told me to return it by fax. In this fast pace, attachment response era we live in, fax return should tell you how basic the operations were. I received a call from the Director some days after the submission in which she offered me the job. Excitement was bursting from within me.

She was looking for an immediate fill date. She wanted to know when I could start. I gave her a two weeks' time frame and told her I needed to provide appropriate parting with the organization I worked for, while that was not her first preference, she understood the distance and permitted me to gather myself and family.

My cousin would say, "You are the only one I know that can get a job and find a place to live over the phone and like it. You do it over and over. I have to give it to you." I would have to tell her, "No, I ask God for the strategy, He just does it so smoothly."

Changing roots, changing fruits, changing lives!
—Patrice Washington

The steps could not have been more ordered. I began searching for a safe community for my children and me to reside. I knew this was the location because I kept changing the search features on different search sites and the same property kept coming up, everything I like and desire in a community. This place was so beautiful to me. The location was amazing. The school district had exceptional ratings and the list goes on and on. So, now it was investigation time. I called the property multiple times. Why would I do that, you may ask? I like to call a location multiple times on different dates at different times of the day to see if I get the same information, I also want to speak with different people. This is my personal method that has proven to work exceptionally well for me. One more thing happened, the location had a move-in-special. Yes, reduction in moving expenses, perfect.

Remember the nice young lady from the employment offer? I needed her assistance again to provide me with proof of employment. However, she didn't stop at providing this information, she told me about the area, proximity to the mall and other entertainment that would help the children transition happily. The apartment would allow me to retain the property with an offer letter of employment. If that wasn't favor, then I don't know what else it would be. I was relocating from another state and the offer letter from the employer was sufficient. That may be the norm there but that would never happen elsewhere, they would want the actual pay stubs. Things are moving forward at an apparent victorious rate. I made the official announcement to my family, friends, and of course, my children. Our squad was not breaking up no matter what. They understood the move and were excited about coming with me this time. After spending some extra time with our loved ones, we immediately focused on packing.

Our items were placed in a storage facility that was close enough to a family residence, that way they could easily monitor our possessions and send items if needed. I told my children if it does not fit in the suitcases, we won't be able to take it. The airline of choice was also part of the strategy. They offered a generous luggage option that we ended up with twelve suitcases, free relocation assistance, as I like to call them. We also found favor with the auto transporter that allowed us to pack the vehicle (things and times have changed so do not try this without asking the transporter if this is allowed). Our vehicle would arrive via auto transport in a few days to a week.

Destiny and anticipation now kissed each other; the morning of set departure had finally arrived. Bright and early before the rising of the sun we were off. We moved in the darkness like thieves getting ready to snatch our destinies. I feel this way because we left from an unfamiliar airport location. We have traveled numerous times but we generally left from the same airport prior. The airport was less congested. The waiting area was unique and nice. The time factor was critical because we wanted to arrive during the early part of the day for the office apartment community so we could get situated. Every part of the trip was like an etch on a bigger canvas. The flight, the arrival into the new city, the weather, it was all beautiful. The air was different and filled with refreshing welcomes in this unknown area. Even the ride from the airport was very peaceful.

Once we arrived at the gated community, I continued to feel excited. I finally got to attach a face with a voice. We were warmly greeted by the office personnel who I had taken a liking to because of her knowledge, promptness, and willingness to help. I really enjoyed how regal the area was. We were now inside a uniquely designed loft-style apartment. No furniture but we had lights, water, and a welcome package from the apartment that consisted of tissue, soap, toothpaste, and other personal effects. We were perfectly positioned for resources. The shopping centers and entertainment areas were literally on the side of the community and across the street. The first acclimation with the move was going to the grocery store. We took the shopping cart from the store lot which was new to me. The community had an area to place the store cart and the store would come and retrieve the carts from the neighborhood. We weren't accustomed to being able or even having a need to remove the shopping cart from the store parking lot. We also walked to our fun destinations, all-new adventures that continued to reveal God's mighty hand upon us. He provided for us in comfort.

Our first night in the apartment tested my creativity to build a pillow. If you use an adult tee-shirt and a few pieces of clothing and fold and lay them inside the adult shirt neatly then tuck the bottom of the shirt and tie the sleeves without making a bump then, you will have a nice, soft pillow. Even though we did not have furniture for the rooms we used them for their intended purposes. We ate our meals in the dining area. I ordered the daily paper not because I was interested in reading the news, but the paper was going to serve many purposes. I would spread the paper on the bathroom floor to step out of the shower, it helped keep the area clean because after the showers they were placed in the recycle bin. The comic section was placed in the dining area for our meals and we used them for additional conversation.

Prior to the vehicle arriving I took them to a children's entertainment center that was literally on the other side of the fence. It was an extreme kids' indoor fun zone area, go-karts, bowling, putt-putt golf, arcade, great food, shout out to that incredible, ooey-gooey pizza, lots of fun and most within walking distance. The vehicle arrived about a week or so later of course with our possessions but it was the television I was waiting for. I bought a very inexpensive television stand from Goodwill; having cable television and the ability to plug in their Xbox would make life easier. The school bus stop was conveniently located across the street from the community.

Not Without My Children

When someone shows you who they are, believe them the first time.

—Maya Angelou

The property assistant provided childcare for my children on a few occasions which was helpful because they didn't have to travel. She introduced us to a college student that wanted a part-time job like the one I was offering. The individual never had to cook, as a matter of fact, they were not permitted to cook for my children. I would make sure that they ate dinner, showered, and had on proper sleepwear before I left for work. These may seem like menial tasks or something the typical babysitter could handle. I wanted my children to be assured that they were my priority. The sole responsibility of the baby-sitter was to provide physical safety for my children. They also did not have to entertain my children, my children had each other, numerous electronics, family, and friends to call and I also called them throughout the night until bedtime. We were the true definition of "watch the children" as adult supervision to ensure their safety, easy money if I may say so. That came to an end when she was relocating out-of-state for the very reason, I needed her and appreciated her. She was offered a live-in nanny position with a wealthy family out-of-state. Gone too fast for my liking.

The hunt for safe and reliable childcare was my next task because I worked the overnight shift. I researched a childcare website and found two individuals. One of which her home was not too far from us. She had great reviews, her home was clean, I observed the children she provided care for. I decided to use her services. My children called me throughout the night. My son was not able to get comfortable because she had two dogs even though they were in the cages at night. I knew then I needed to look for another childcare resource urgently and this came faster than I intended when I picked my children up in the morning and my daughter said that the dog chased her brother and he was terrified running in the community. She said some of the adults were trying to calm him down. Even though she provided good care I was not going to subject my children to the terror of a dog, I would not let that happen, God has always given me favor with my children and the care of them.

*A happy heart makes the face cheerful, but
heartache crushes the spirit.*
—*Proverbs 15:13 NIV*

The next person who provided care was a respiratory therapist who worked at the hospital with me. That was cool at least they were medically inclined if needed and they also knew exactly how to find me besides my cell phone, right. I call this long-distance care. We would have to leave our city four hours earlier than when I needed to start work because I was going to have to take them almost two hours away. The traffic on this highway always came to a standstill at a particular time which I inevitably had to get around, and like valiant soldiers, they got their bags and we headed out.

Pause right here, because we spent so much time in the vehicle together, I had talking books and other activities for them. We were maximizing every moment and to this day, we have a cheer that I used to do with them in the car when it was getting too quiet or I wanted to add a little fun in the car. I would say, "Where my babies at?" They would respond, "right here" I would say that twice. Then I would say, "somebody, anybody make some noiiiiiisssseeee!!!" and they would start screaming until I closed my hand like they do with the choir. It was so funny and just broke the dullness at times, just fun. It is so good to laugh with my children. They liked this spot because she had two children; a boy and a girl, of the same order, close in age that they could play with.

I will tell anyone that when you have a hunger and desire to achieve, you absolutely can. The path is filled with many turns and having an aptness to hear from God will be vital to not only surviving but ultimately thriving in all areas of your life and for those associated with you. That was a temporary fix because the drive was not something I wanted to endure for an extended period of time because I would arrive at work and have to take a nap in my car before the start of my shift but it was necessary and greatly appreciated at the time.

We are less lonely when we connect.
—Nikki Giovanni

Look around, look around. Open your eyes wide and see the many resources that are before you. I realized that in an eatery, breakfast done right and fast was just what I needed. I could tell the numerous times Denny's served as my personal chef and respite. I would pick my children up from the overnight care provider and stop at Denny's. Way too exhausted to dine with them, I took them inside and ordered their meals. They both had cellular phones and were instructed to call me when they finished eating and wanted to come outside. These instructions were necessary because I was going to be in the car taking as long a nap as possible while they enjoyed their meals. The server also knew the instructions for them.

I can't stress the need for staying in tune with God especially about your children. I am not saying that I always understood the entire plan, but I took the steps in the directions that I heard to go. We visited another childcare person even though I was not going to need her services soon because I had communicated with my manager that childcare was not solidified to my comfort. He allowed me to maneuver my schedule. There was another provider from the childcare website. Her home was also clean, but I remember thinking about our conversation and getting this unsettling feeling in my stomach.

As the days went on, I still rehearsed our conversation in my head until one night I had a dream about the conversation and I heard clear as day, "do not take the children over there, do not let her watch your children." I woke up and could still hear the small, still voice instructing me not to let her provide care for the children. She called me a few days before the time I told her I would need her services. I told her that we had decided not to use her services. She said that her daughter could pick my children up. I further declined her offer and I believe she offered two additional times. No thanks and I concluded the conversation. It was like a cool refreshing breeze came over me once I finished speaking with her.

Ask for what you want and be prepared to get it.
—*Maya Angelou*

I tend to get on my soapbox about how sometimes the very resources we need are so close to us, but we overlook them. I was driving down the same street I had traveled multiple times during the week and saw that a church was offering early morning childcare. It was yet another time to kick into my research mode to call the service provider or intended organization multiple times of the day on different days to see if I received the same knowledgeable and warm service. I even called from the parking lot. So far so good, I toured the facility without my children then I went back with them. The only steppingstone was the times of services that opened during normal business hours, in this case, 6 am-7 pm. But normal was not what I needed. I needed to be at my clinicals that took over an hour to get to, by 7 am without any exceptions.

Continuing on this ordered path, the receptionist informed me that she always arrives early and was willing to supervise my children if I didn't mind them having to sit in the lobby for thirty-minutes with her as she prepared her work area, then they could go into the childcare center. Just like soldiers, 4:30 a.m. alarms and exiting the house no later than 5:15 a.m. Right here, I have to express an overwhelming thanks to my children who never complained about the schedule. They were flexible and exuded love to me. This place would drop them to school and another after school provider would pick them up. The afterschool daycare was another place of excellence. I worked in the area and would always see how the families and kids looked so excited to be going in there. At first, I thought it was probably because they have a pool and the children can enjoy it with supervision. Yes, that could certainly be an added joy for the children but for me, as the parent, I experienced friendly, timely staff that observed the children through direct supervision and cameras. That was very comforting to me. This arrangement continued for as long as it was necessary, for us necessity changed frequently because of my academic classes with the clinicals. The clinical sites are limited, and location of course could not be guaranteed. We have made it through another successful semester, but the church daycare was going to be removed.

> *If you're always trying to be normal you will never know how amazing you can be.*
> —*Maya Angelou*

    I can't pen this book without interruption because as I scribe the journey of us as a family, I have to stop and say thank you. Thank you God for the abundance of grace that was continuously poured upon me and my children. Chuck E. Cheese was my library. Why would I say that? I am glad you are pondering. As a single parent, I didn't want my children to have to sacrifice their childhood experiences and fun because I was pursuing a second-degree, change of career. Learning about how to be resourceful, in my paper, the home décor mats bundle were also coupons from Chuck E. Cheese.

    To make the best use of this fun zone childcare provider you make sure that the children have had a great breakfast and just about the time they have digested you head on over to the fun spot. When we got there, I would get the table in the corner that was generally located to a clear view of the facility to include the food and the door. We would place the order together, but I would instruct them not to make it until I came back, or they came back and said they were ready for the order to be made. They could play until it was lunchtime. They ate during my break time so I could eat with them, then they went back to playing and I returned to studying. The manager would come over and ask how I could study in such a noisy place.

I informed him that it was a different type of noise and I could easily block it out. I could only hear my children. It worked out great by the time the coins were completed we would have been there at least four to six hours, which to a child is a cool day; fun, pizza, and more fun. It was a win, win situation for me. I was able to get some focused study time so that once we returned home, I could be present with them for dinner and a cartoon or movie and still get to bed at a decent hour of the night.

CHAPTER 3
WE'RE BETTER TOGETHER

Let's not forget that I still needed to find a new childcare provider. You know the routine, research mode time. Let's go! I contacted an in-home, family, twenty-four hours, and weekend provider. I remember thinking that this conversation seemed different. It was more like I had called a friend to watch the kids for me. She invited us over to her home. We all went to receive the tour at the same time. Yes, yes, yes! The maternal instincts, the safety, the love was felt, her children were welcoming, and my kids just acclimated immediately. Just like I felt on the phone. They were playing for so long as she and I talked we hadn't realized how much time had elapsed.

So, remember, I said the church childcare was ending, how about this new provider, also ended the afterschool pick-up as she was willing to come and pick the children up. This was great because I preferred for my children to be back in the home as soon after school as possible so that they could get situated since they were such early risers, not by choice but by love.

    We saw each other even on the weekends and took our kids to fun places together. This was the childcare provider that ended all the searches. The childcare provider that has blossomed into a close family relationship. I had many helpers along the way to success because it is a journey, not a sprint.

CHAPTER 4
I'VE GOT YOU COVERED

Working the overnight shift while attending morning classes was a daunting task not only emotionally, physically but also hygienic. The solution to a problem I had was the infamous mesh underwear that came in handy the very few times I forgot to put a clean pair of underwear in my uniform pocket. I even had pairs in my glove compartment, but time was of the essence in the morning and I was too busy providing patient care to go outside to my car to retrieve mine. I had my own but on the rare occasions I had not packed additional underwear I would ask the mother-baby unit for the mesh underwear. I was short of time once I got off work before classes started. So, I took my lunch break as closest to getting off shift as I could so that I could prepare myself in the bathroom for classes. Looking back, everything seemed like another creative, resourceful strategy on how to view my action.

CHAPTER 5
BLUR

Out the door as soon as my relief arrived, they would be on time, something I appreciated then and I have learned to appreciate and practice in my report giving. The morning needed to flow like a cool stream because I had to maneuver traffic to get to classes on time. The morning seemed like a blur to me. I literally had a headache every day of class. The teacher was a big blur to me. I was retaining the information but looking forward to the hour lunch break we were given, this time was not for eating, but for sleeping. I called my friends and mom back in Florida to let them know that I was going to sleep in the car and to please wake me up. I also set my clock and placed the phone far enough from me that I literally would have to get up to silence the alarm. Time management at its best, really, why should I try to eat something when the instructor permitted you to eat in class if it didn't have a strong odor and wasn't a six-course meal.

I'M YOUR PUSHER

Can two walk together, unless they are agreed?
—Amos 3:3 NKJV

    A warm greeting to a stranger has cultivated into a genuine likeness for each other and kindness for our families. A few semesters into the program the instructor gave us a pep talk about being kind to the new students that would be joining the class at this juncture. She did not want us to get irritated when we arrived to class and someone was sitting in our seats. You and I know that many people are creatures of habits and will innately assign themselves seats and it is then just understood that no one should sit in their assigned seats. Yeah, I laugh at this just like you did because we have found ourselves on both the receiving and giving end of this action. On this particular day when I arrived to class, almost everyone was already present. As I proceeded to go to my seating area, I saw an unfamiliar face and so I greeted her. She was sitting down, and while I was still standing, she looked up at me, her face looked like she wanted to cry. She asked me if she could give me a hug, I agreed with my thoughts rapidly going as to why would a total stranger ask a total stranger for a hug and even more concerning, why did I agree? She said this class is almost full and you were the only person to say hello to me. She went on to tell me of her victory over a medical condition that had prevented her from finishing with her class and she had finally received clearance to finish the pursuit of her dreams. We encouraged each other for the rest of the class, I actually started eating lunch with her during our break time and we sat by each other in class and looked, laughed, and awaited the end of school, of course.

That moment in time has blossomed into a valuable friendship I have even until this day. At graduation, her family came over to me and thanked me for my kindness towards her. We stayed in touch with each other even after I returned to Florida. She was the first person to come visit us when we came back to Texas to pursue my registered nursing degree and she brought so many items with her. From a bookshelf, dining table, and living room tables, microwave, kitchen glassware, etc. I told her our furniture was coming in about a month because of long haul travel. I wouldn't have imagined she was going to bring all these housewarming gifts. She attended my graduation. The wonderful friendship didn't stop there, we would enjoy monthly breakfast meetups to catch up and laugh, we still talk to this very day. Your pause can create a story. This is also a great example of pouring into someone's life without any expectations of compensation.

As I am writing, I am realizing I reaped an abundance of furniture because I have sown an abundance of furniture. My mom says every time you move you buy new furniture. I remember I had these custom couches and I was moving. My mom said, "I know you are not taking them with you." I said, "No, if the movers want them, they can have them or anybody who can get them out the door is welcome to take and enjoy them." I always have something that I offer the movers to take and they are usually astonished that someone would give those items up. I don't give anything that I wouldn't want to receive. I've learned the value of sowing and reaping.

I'M YOUR PUSHER

All great achievements require time.
—Maya Angelou

The day that snuck up on me was our actual academic classes which were complete, we were just getting advice for the pinning ceremony. I had never missed a day of classes so I decided that I was going to go ahead and pick up a shift that day at work, a personal sitter case, that couldn't be any easier at this time. As I was at work, I started getting text messages informing me that I was nominated by my peers to deliver the speech at our nursing pinning ceremony. This meant speaking in front of a large crowd of people I didn't know. I was like, I am not doing this as I continued to stare at the text messages before I responded to anyone. Lots of thoughts went through my head as to which one of my peers started that. I will keep that to myself. Now I do not know if this was because no one else wanted to or how they figured I should do it. There was one person in class that would tell me the truth of what was happening and just at the moment I thought to call her, she called me. I said, yeah, I saw the text, how did this come to be? I told her the name of our peer that I thought nominated me, and she said yes, but it was the professor first. Really?!? Why?!? Okay I guess.

If you are around me long enough you will discover that I don't voluntarily say much. I am fine with listening. A statement I often say is, I have two ears and one mouth, and I like that ratio. I am a good listener. This was not something I was going to take lightly, so I took it to God in prayer. I requested the class roster and all of the clinical sites everyone attended. This speech needed to be personal and personable to allow everyone to see where they started and acknowledge the accomplishment of where they were and embrace where they were going.

> *Her mouth speaks from that which fills her heart.*
> *—Luke 6:45*

Two revelatory discussions are going to be seen here:

1) The actual finalization of my speech with the academic institution removed.
2) My detailed thought process of the speech.

Acknowledgment:

Good Evening faculty, families, friends, and graduating class. It is with great privilege and honor that I stand before everyone to speak on our behalf.

"It was the best of times, it was the worst of times, it was the age of wisdom, it was the age of foolishness, it was the epoch of belief, it was the epoch of incredulity, it was the season of Light, it was the season of Darkness, it was the spring of hope, it was the winter of despair, we had everything before us, we had nothing before us…."

—Charles Dickens

Invitation:

How many of us can recall the luncheon we attended prior to the start of school? It was a setup to let us know this would probably be our last and most complete meal that we could chew slowly until we graduated.

Studies:

To our families who encouraged us to stay up and study for yet another critical thinking test, of course, while they went to sleep. Who can forget Pharmacology, as much as we would like to forget? It's one of those subjects that make you say why? why? why? but just like pharmacology was here to stay, so were we, so we just buckled down and decided to become intimate friends.

Issues:

As much as we wanted the clock to stand still and our daily lives to make a straight line, it did not. Life happened while we pursued our calling. Some of us had to overcome physical illnesses in our own bodies, yet still, we arose to the occasion. Others had to juggle unreliable childcare, yet still, we arose to the occasion. Others even learned how to become expert financial managers as they had to decrease working hours or even resign yet still, we arose to the occasion. Others traveled from distances as far as Hill Country in pursuit of our calling.

Preparation:

The steps of a prudent nurse are truly ordered by dedicated, knowledgeable, and caring faculty. The faculty and staff here at our nursing school are second to none; they are seasoned in their specialties. There is a sense of a family here. We shared our tragedies in hopes of bringing triumph to others. Office hours were made readily available, technology also works, send an email, or a text. You will receive a response, instructions, and an action plan.

No stones were left unturned, no squeaky areas without oil. Our pursuits were individualized through an action plan.

Our professors reviewed our test scores, our retention of information, our strengths, and our areas for improvement. For once, yes, it really was all about YOU!

As students, we also had a voice through the Student Nurse Association (SNA) and the Student Government

The foundation we stand on at our nursing school is solid ground.

Clinical site experiences:

The extensive clinical experiences were also an integral part of our preparation. The various clinical sites we had to travel to because we had to be there by 6:45 am, yes that is in the morning after all hospitals are open twenty-four hours a day. On our way to Mission Trail Baptist Hospital, we wondered how many hospitals we passed along the way? The telemetry and medical-surgical staff all embraced us, so the distance quickly faded away. Main Baptist downtown, could easily be referred to as a clinical buffet that consists of the rehab unit, the renal unit, outpatient services, over to the operating room ending with the mother-baby unit.

Our leadership skills were developed on the psychiatric unit, to evolve out of a quiet, reserved state, to a decision-maker. The chiseling out of prudent nurses continued to Northeast Baptist cardiovascular unit and G.I. lab over to North Central Baptist with the Stroke Fair. The nursing homes offered the optimal code brown experiences. We continued to put our hands to the plow with Project Measure Up's Health Awareness Initiative. So, whether it is being able to stomach an invasive procedure, or endure the smell of C-Diff, we did it, like "champs."

NCLEX you defeated foe, as we remember our ABC's, then attacked you safely, we earned a star.

Future:

As we close this chapter of our lives, we also embark on a new adventurous journey of bringing hope and healing not only to our patients but their family members. We are an integral part of our own neighborhood, the community, and society at large.

"It was the best of times, it was the worst of times…"

We have developed into prudent nurses here at our nursing school, "where caring is your calling".

Thank you for this humbling experience.

Out of the abundance of the heart the mouth speaks.
—Luke 6:45

I purposely wrote in sections because I wanted to make sure that I gave attention to everyone. I requested a class roster from the instructors and a list of clinical sites. I felt it was an honor to represent the class and I wanted to personalize it so that they could recognize themselves easily in the speech. The opening quote by Charles Dickens spoke volumes because of the duality that we were definitely enduring throughout the program. This duality became evident shortly after beginning the program. We were enticed and offered a beautifully catered meal in which the educational faculty, hospital managers, and directors were in attendance. The smiles displayed were that of excitement and counsel to steady yourself for a journey that was going to definitely challenge you but because of the nature of the calling, don't take it personal, the actions are rooted in public safety. We were given hope of having employment at the end because these same individuals would be at many of the clinical sites. It was a rather good set-up. The set was thorough and flawless.

This was the start of a journey that impacted our entire lives, including our families. Our families indeed sacrificed and that is not to be taken lightly whenever you endeavor to take your family to the next level no matter what the industry. It is vital that you include them in the decision making as much as possible and as is age-appropriate. Also, don't forget to factor in their schedules. Some subjects just stand out like a sore thumb, it is understood that they demand and declare that you keep them on the front page, pharmacology is definitely one of those master subjects that there isn't any in-between. So as pharmacology was there to stay so were we.

I also thought it was fitting to mention our physical battles. Terminal illness or any disease processes that affect your health can be emotionally and physically draining. I am better at it now. But over the years whenever I had a task that was going to be physically challenging because of the hours, I would change not only my eating habits but those of my children. They were the immediate people that I could not afford to get sick especially if it was related to a modified behavior. It should go without saying, but never compromise the safety of your children. I assure you, you won't be able to concentrate on the task if you didn't receive peace about your decision, to say the least, that unreliable childcare is an understatement.

In nursing school three things related to your diet changes: 1.) You stop being able to eat those fancy meals that require you to pay attention as you bring the food to your mouth. Pocket snacks and non-messy fruits become your nutritional support. 2.) You forget to eat until it is necessary. Your food bill shrinks. 3.) Now you may either gain or lose weight, to each his own on that note. As far as employment, some voluntarily quit their positions or receive the official notification to relieve their position, I prefer the earlier selection. Of course, you're reading the story of how I physically relocated from another state. Some of my classmates had to travel for more than an hour in one direction to get to class on time. The inclement weather, sick loved ones, and transportation issues can't be in your weekly excuse rotation while in nursing school.

Please do not enter a nursing program, or any educational institution for that matter, with an expectation that faculty must like you as an individual. They are there to respectfully provide you with the knowledge required to help you attain your goals. For me, I was fortunate that I was in a school where the professors and administrators cared about us personally. This was evident because they would frequently ask about those who were working, childcare, and basic things which was not expected but greatly appreciated. I am one to believe that respect and distance should be retained between students and instructors while the courses are going on.

Our clinical site experiences truly thrust us into the real world of nursing and taught us things we probably wish we did not have to learn. One such thing was code brown. I would not want anyone to be unclear about what code brown was. It is feces. Some bowel movements have a distinct, ferocious smell that immediately helps you to identify the culprit, one for sure is clostridium difficile -aka C-diff. We not only gained knowledge at the clinical sites, but we were given the opportunity to pour back into the community with different health fairs.

"Champ" refers to me and what happened at my clinical site. I was going into an invasive procedure in which you had to put on a lead shield. I applied the shield to include the thyroid portion. We were not quite ready to begin. So, I started feeling hot, so I shifted my stance from leg to leg. Then there was a chair close by, I said you know I think I will just sit over here until we are ready. The nurses asked me if I was ok. I said yes, I just feel very hot, but I am going to have a sit down right here until we are ready. They called my clinical instructor and they said it is the shield, it took them a while to get used to it. Of course, the instructor had to briefly leave another group that she was with to come and get me from the operating room. So, we returned together and apparently, I looked flush. A classmate started saying, "oh you handled that like a champ." It was meant as an insult, but I totally ignored the remarks. Since then I have been in procedures that require this and I am fine, so yes, I handled it like a champ.

I was vigilant throughout my studies because I had the end in mind. There was a gatekeeper of a test waiting because you can take all the classes you want, pay the fees, receive clearance to test and not pass the boards and you cannot legally practice. That obviously would be devastating and discouraging. The day of reckoning had arrived. There is no way of knowing exactly what they are going to ask but through prayer and preparation, I passed my boards the first time around. It was truly a humbling experience.

Upon completion of my speech, I thanked the assembly, bowed, and went to exit the stage when a standing ovation and an uproar of claps erupted. I was thoroughly surprised and humbled that my genuine speech was received well. So many people came up to me after graduation and told me how powerful my speech was. Some people even recorded it. I tried to maintain my focus when I saw that occurring during my speech. I even had more mature people in their professions stating that experienced executives do not deliver speeches in such an excellent manner. One of the most memorable comments came from a gentleman who had been the valedictorian when he graduated from college. He said his speech was nowhere near as powerful as my speech. I thanked him and then continued to take memorable pictures with the people who had allowed me to represent them. I am even more thankful for what God had accomplished through me. I was exceedingly joyful as my children pinned me at the ceremony with a beautiful nurse pin my mom had sent. My mom could not attend the pinning ceremony but was arriving for graduation.

> *They may forget your name but they will never forget how you made them feel.*
> —Maya Angelou

Laughter and the smell of food filled the corridor of the nursing school. They were back, the charming, welcoming crew from the luncheon we attended prior to the start of school. Now that we had graduated, we were able to enjoy this meal together and chew slowly once again. This time they came bearing gifts of opportunities to be employed in their hospitals and on their units.

I absolutely wanted the opportunity to work in an acute care hospital setting and I received such an opportunity from the medical-surgical/oncology unit director. This was going to be a new venture in uncharted territory. I showed up for my first day of work looking like a newborn. My hair was in place, clothing crisp, and I had a sponge-like attitude, ready to learn from the greatest. I was fortunate to have a knowledgeable, patient, and flexible mentor and an engaged educator that allowed me to implement what I was taught within the operational guidelines. I can say that not one day in nursing is the same, even if you work on the same unit. The characteristics of the patients, families, and staff are like a smorgasbord. It is all in there and makes up the total recipe, which is the patient care experience.

I'M YOUR PUSHER

*Seek God's will in all you do, and he will show you
the path to take.*

—*Proverbs 3:6*

With a couple of months of acute care training experience under my belt, I made the decision to return to Florida. Note very carefully - I made the decision. In the hype and hysteria of obtaining my Licensed Vocational Nursing (LVN) certification, I decided to move and did not consult God about this to find out if this was the right move or the right time. Let me say this again, I did not consult God. I had goals of continuing to obtain my Registered Nursing degree and was handed a great opportunity at graduation by leadership, but I declined.

I thought I was better positioned and could easily pick back up in Florida, doing a bridge education program. We packed up our belongings and headed south. What a rude awakening I experienced by returning to Florida, thinking I would be able to provide a comfortable lifestyle for my family since becoming a licensed vocational nurse. So, at this time, there are states that are what I have termed licensed vocational nurse or licensed practical nurse friendly states. Unfortunately, according to my personal experience, Florida was not one of them.

Let me illustrate the differences. While in Texas, I was able to command a decent hourly rate as an LVN. The hospitals employed LVNs as well as skilled nursing facilities, nursing homes, rehabilitation centers, etc. You really could thrive financially as well as academically with such an affordable cost of living. The opportunities seemed endless. Florida, on the other hand, I was not able to locate any hospitals that hired licensed vocational/practical nurses. The LVNs had been long time employees and were being encouraged to pursue their registered nursing degree in a specific time, or they faced being terminated. This was the big push for the hospital to obtain magnet status. The nursing homes did not have any openings.

I did find favor with a nursing executive that was willing to provide me with a hospital position but, I was not willing to travel so far in South Florida traffic, especially when I would have to deal with Interstate 95-South. This was when I was introduced to home health care nursing; what a great way to have your own time. I was able to make my own schedule but traveled in my own vehicle extensively. I was taking so many assignments and enjoying the job, but the mountainous paperwork was not appealing to me. It began to take more time to complete while I was home.

Once I sat down and figured out how much I was making with the drive, the paperwork, and the maintenance of a luxury vehicle, I decided I needed to have an exit plan.

CHAPTER 6
WALK IT OUT

    I am so glad I serve the God of a second chance and many more when I reflect on my life. However, we are going to discuss my second chance. It was time to continue my education most expeditiously. I applied to nursing schools back in Texas. Why not Florida, you may ask. I was always looking at schools in Florida schools, and just like before, they had an even greater waitlist for the bridge programs. I was definitely not doing that. I already had an open-door that I had declined. I applied there and to another school. I was accepted into both. I chose a different school based on my family requirements, but I was able to be re-hired at my former employer. A sweatless victory was what I experienced every time I applied in Texas. It was apparent to me and my family we would be leaving Florida again.

I'M YOUR PUSHER

Hold onto your dreams.
—Langston Hughes

It came as no surprise when I told my family we are heading back to Texas. Here comes my cousin again, she would say, "You are the only one I know that can get a job, find a place over the phone and it will be as if you had gone there in person. I have to give it to you." This time I had a memory recall to work with. I would have to tell her, "No, I ask God for the strategy, He just does it so smoothly". This time I was familiar with the areas. Interesting when we first resided in Texas, there was a community that I said I was going to relocate us to once my lease was up. Instead, we returned to Florida. So, for this move, I searched for the community name on-line, contacted them, and was greeted with excellent customer service every time. I was able to obtain the last three-bedroom they had. This was important to me because I wanted my children to have their own rooms. I gathered the team and auto-transport carrier which had now moved my vehicle multiple times.

We arrived in Texas with the same welcome we had known before. The driver loaded our belongings into the van and started to take us to our apartment. We noticed that he didn't turn on the street I knew the community was on. He kept going across the highway. My kids and I stared at each other. We arrived at a nice community, okay. I searched for the apartment community by name and city then I contacted the rental office. Yes, this was our address. It never occurred to me that there may be another community with the same name. The associate directed us to our apartment. It was huge, it took up one side of the building, and only four apartments were on the entire floor. The lights were on and everything was in full swing. Our belongings would arrive by truck and of course, the vehicle was on its way. Once my children picked their rooms, we headed to the car rental center. It was more cost-effective to take a taxi to the rental place from our apartment than the airport because our excess luggage would make us need a more expensive vehicle until my SUV arrived. We were interested in finding out what had happened with the property mix-up.

We drove to the other location and the community had changed its name, no wonder. This place was not that far from our previous residence which was also not far from the airport. However, this new community was also perfectly located for us. We did not need any childcare coverage. I was no longer working the brutal, night-shift. An added bonus was that the bus stop was on the same side of the streets for the times they would need it. Everything was coming together.

And we know all things work together for the good to them that love God.

—Romans 8:28

CHAPTER 7
DIABOLICAL SCHEDULE

It seemed as though I had a different job or shift each semester. To me, without question, the most diabolic schedule is the one-two-one shift. I am going to paint a vivid picture for you. I attended classes Monday through Friday as usual with traditional classes. I made valiant attempts of being ready for my shifts by Thursday, but here comes Friday like it always does. I would come home and make sure my children saw all of their meals and snacks that were prepared. The goal of Friday evening was to get in bed as fast as I could because I would be leaving for work soon. Round one, I would go to work on Friday night at 10 pm and get off work at 6 am, which really meant 7 am by the time the report was completed.

I used Friday's one- hour lunch breaks to review the previous class assignments for the week and review the coming assignments. When I got off on Saturday morning, I would call my kids to make sure they unlocked the door for me. If they didn't pick up and I was really tired I would just sleep in my vehicle. I didn't want to disturb their sleep or startle them coming into the house at that time of the morning, especially on the weekend. If I was hungry, I would just go to Denny's. Once they realized I had called, they called me back and told me to come home. Round two, I must return to work on Saturday for a 2 pm-10 pm then a 10 pm-6 am shift. Oh man, this is where women against sleep deprivation fight. The lunch breaks had to be maximized. Since it was essentially two shifts back to back, I got two one-hour lunch breaks. The first break I would go home and eat lunch with my children. I would sometimes surprise them with delivery to arrive by the time I got there. I used the second break to study. I finally got off on Sunday at 6 am, well 7 am roughly by the time shift report is over.

Oooooh weeee, sleep time! I call my kids right before I drive off. Yes, they pick up. I greet my kids, shower, and bed here I come. The last hurrah is Sunday because I must return to work for a 2 pm-10 pm shift. During this shift's one-hour break I headed home to make sure my kids were ready for school on Monday. Finally, 10 pm comes, having completed my report, it is submitted early. I was usually happy about this shift handoff because that nurse usually came early.

This was intense but hopeful because I knew I did not have to come back until next Friday. This went on for the entire semester, two whole months. I did not want my kids to be waiting up for me because they had school the next day. It did not seem to bother them at all, of course. I would call my children right before I left the parking lot and then it was home sweet home with my lovely children and my bed. The funniest thing is I think this is the shift that literally taught me the meaning of jumping in my bed. To this day, my daughter cannot stop laughing at me after I have worked a long shift and I am exhausted, apparently, I get in the bed differently. I did not realize she had observed that. Basic tired gets "sit on the side of the bed, put your feet up" kind of deal. Exhausted tired gets, "I cannot wait to get to bed, run, jump and pull the cover over you in one move" kind of deal. It is hilarious when I think about it.

CHAPTER 8
DOUBLE WEEKENDS

New semester, new job, and one step closer to graduation but the shifts did not get any easier. Who comes up with these schedules for people much less nursing students? The Double-Double sounds good for ice-cream or cake. This is the story of no more weekends for a while. So much so my coworker and I would dance down the long hallways to a song that was entitled, "Double-Double." From one-two-one, now I was working Saturday from 6 am-10 pm, which unfortunately meant closer to midnight with all the charting. It was also the same timing on Sunday, closer to midnight. I couldn't help waking my children up at times until I figured that if I called them at 10 pm on Sundays only, right before they went to bed and I asked them to take off the top lock so I could get in the house they did not do that often, they just waited up for me. In turn, I took them to school as much as I possibly could.

I really enjoyed taking and dropping my kids off at school; that served as great encouragement for me with this shift, and once again creativity had to come into play. There could possibly be time to study while working if I calculated it. The residents had activity time and nap time. So, staying focused and ahead of the task was crucial. Having tests on Mondays was a bit much. So, I found a friend, a PRN (Pro Re Nata, a Latin phrase that translates to as needed) worker who was faithful in keeping his word and was looking to earn extra cash to purchase his dream vehicle, a great opportunity for us. I would ask him to cover the Sunday, 2-10 pm portion of my shift. Please do not overlook anyone or assume anything, you absolutely do not know what people are willing to do for you from a genuine position. He never asked for anything in return.

> *However, as it is written: that no eye has seen, what no ear has heard and what no human mind has conceived – the things God has prepared for those who love Him.*
>
> —1 Corinthians 2:9

Clear skies, little to no traffic was the forecast early on a Saturday morning as I was taking my friend to work. When out of nowhere this vehicle hit my Lexus truck so hard that the vehicle sent my vehicle into hydroplane on the normally busy freeway. It was apparent they did not intend on stopping because when my vehicle stopped spinning and I was turned facing traffic at this point they hit me again, only this time their vehicle got stuck under my tire area. This time they ended up dragging me across the highway into the ditch just short of hitting the guard rails.

I remember telling my friend to please call my mom on his phone because I could not reach my phone. I told him, "I cannot feel my left side and my head hurts." Yes, we were wearing our seatbelts that goes without saying when you get into my vehicle. That includes your baby as well. No car seat then we will need to get theirs or purchase one or you're not riding. He called my mom, she said, "You know I almost didn't answer because I don't know this number but because I saw the Texas area code I answered." The first thing I told her was that I was ok and that I couldn't feel my left side and my head hurts. I could feel the fear that gripped her. I told her he had already called the ambulance.

The people who hit me were in the ditch also because they were stuck to my vehicle and that I can't really turn to see them because they were on my left. She asked where the kids were. I told her that I left them at the house because my daughter had just fallen asleep after being up all night and I had recently given her a treatment. My son was in the room with her because I called him out of his room to stay with her just in case, she needed anything. I was very thankful because had I not given my daughter the treatment, I would have had them with me. My son would normally sit behind me. That would have been disastrous because the side they hit me on and got stuck by was my front driver tire area. I was stuck in my vehicle. Once the ambulance arrived, one of them got in the vehicle while the other one was outside. He ended up having to crack the door. They did put the neck brace on, as I told him my head was hurting and I couldn't feel my left side. They and my friend just about carried me to the stretcher because of how we were positioned in the ditch. The other driver said sorry as they were leading me to the stretcher.

My blood pressure was off the charts. They whisked me away to the nearest hospital. I was familiar with the hospital because I previously worked there and had clinicals there. I felt pain everywhere on my right. Now I am self-diagnosing in my mind because we were in the neurological section of class. I notified my professor as soon as I came from the hospital that day. I had no intention of missing class on Monday regardless of my accident. My vehicle was taken in and I was provided a rental vehicle that I couldn't drive because of my headache and lack of feeling. I put my friend on the rental and his name on my insurance. I found out it wouldn't cost me anything additional to do that as this was my first experience with this.

At that time, I had two nursing friends that stayed with us during the week to attend classes because they lived two to four hours away. I relaxed the best way I could. I spent time with my children and took the medication that knocked me out. Here comes Monday, class time. My friends had it all worked out. Originally, I was the one helping them out, but they came through for me also. I had early classes, one friend had mid-morning classes and the other had late classes. They configured a schedule that included me. The one with the late classes would take me to class literally all the way to my seat with my books and the mid-morning drove me home, or the late would come back and pick me up. I timed the medication perfectly so that I could be alert in class. This went on for about a month until I started physical therapy. That was a whole other feat, two-to-three times a week. I had to study so guess what, I had my recordings playing in my ear once the physical therapist gave me the planned activities.

It certainly was not easy with my neck being in so much pain and I often had sharp, shooting pain in my back. The feeling to my left would intermittently return. The individual who hit me, the driver did not have a license and the passenger who was the owner of the vehicle did not have insurance. This was all made known to me by my insurance company; they provided the accident officer with their insurance card as we know it shows the range of coverage not if it is active. Unfortunately, my insurance company totaled my vehicle out. They gave me a minuscule check of $500, which I first gave an offering on, sent my mom a few dollars, bought myself some new high heels, and gave my kids an even amount. The expenses from this no-fault of my own accident did not stop. I had to personally pay for rental cars for almost four months of which my dad graciously footed the bill to provide reliable transportation for us. God always had a plan.

I was not going to purchase a vehicle that I did not want just to get rid of having to rent a vehicle. My favorite vehicle has always been the BMW, so naturally, I started to look at these vehicles. I also started looking at another luxury line maker that was close to the house. I do not like to be harassed when I am shopping. If I came to the store, then I am interested and I know how to get your attention once you have introduced yourself. The lot was not gated, and they did not open on Sundays, perfect time to vehicle shop. I was not the only one that had that same thought, there were regulars there on Sundays. I had a plethora of beautiful vehicles that my children and I had looked at.

I was out of town when I received this belligerent phone call from the rental place stating that I owed them this exorbitant amount of money. The new manager who was there for about a week called me from his personal phone spewing inaccurate information. I said, "What are you talking about, sir? I have been renting here for almost four months straight and I have never met you. I change the vehicles all the time because if I am going to rent then I want to try all the vehicles out." He said, "Well I am newly assigned here and I have looked at your records." I assured him he was in absolute error and mentioned some other people who worked there that he should consult with once he checked his story at the office and not be calling a consistent customer from his personal phone without having access to the records. He went on and on. I will have to pick up the vehicle. I told him I am out of town, do what you want to do. You know the address just make sure that you are one hundred percent accurate when I get back because I will be calling corporate right in front of you. I am on vacation and you need one. Have a great day and then I ended the call.

I had a contact at one of the dealers I had reviewed because I went to test drive the vehicle. I looked on-line and oh, there was a beauty that I had not seen on the lot. I called the service representative and he kept saying he walked a lot yesterday and he didn't see it. I said no, it's there and that's the vehicle I want. He said he was going to take another look and call me back. In a very short time, he called me back and said he didn't know when that vehicle arrived. He walked the lot and it was not there. I said it was hidden for me so that's the one I want. The entire sweatless transaction was done on the phone while I was out of town. He asked me what my flight arrangement was. The morning we headed to the airport, the dealership called me and said give them a call when I got home. I arrived at my house; the rental company had retrieved their vehicle as the belligerent manager stated. The dealership sales representative came to the house to pick me up in the top of the line model they had in one of their other trucks.

Customer service was stellar. I signed my papers, my insurance company faxed the coverage, and my vehicle was already washed, detailed, and exquisitely parked under the tent. We got in the car, he gave me a tour and the deal were solidified. I experienced a sweat less transaction, unparalleled customer service, and received a high-performance vehicle that all came from the favor of God. I drove my vehicle to the rental place to get my items that were left in the car. They all greeted me of course because I was not a stranger. I requested to speak with the belligerent manager, who, unsurprisingly, didn't work there anymore. I took my items and got in my beautiful gift. Bye rental folks!

For the weapons of our warfare are not carnal, but mighty through God to the pulling down of strongholds.
— *2 Corinthians 10:4 KJV*

Almost at the end, why introduce an exit test that has nothing to do with the boards? I take my studies profoundly seriously. I did not miss one day of class. If you spend any amount of time with me you know I have plans for the plans when it comes to implementing studying, it includes bathroom breaks, meals, and making and returning phone calls. If any of the items don't happen in the allotted time frame it just has to wait until the next scheduled occurrence. There was this exit test trying to block my release. I don't have test anxiety. I must have reviewed a couple thousand practice questions for sure because the instructor and the class were keeping records. I took the test twice and didn't pass. Even the instructors were stunned and in disbelief. It is one thing to know a person doesn't study and see the negative results, it's a totally different ache to know the opposite and get the same negative results.

I had one more chance to do what my counselor advised. I went to my car and I cried so hard that I couldn't drive. Maybe an hour later one of my friends called to check on me and find out where I was. I told her I was still in the parking lot. She came over and sat in the car with me. She encouraged me as she knew how I studied, we studied together. I even tutored. I couldn't figure this out. I even went to see the school psychologist they had as a resource for us. The next step I took was the barrier breaker. I had a classmate that we had fasted throughout the semester for her family. Now we were about to go into attack mode about this test. We decided to fast for a two-week period so that this attack would be removed. Whatever hindrance was there was defeated now. There was no way this was a natural attack, it had to be spiritual with an absolute demonic presence. There was no way, I repeat no way, that this God who is too faithful to fail would allow me to move across the state, change time zones, get admitted into numerous schools, orchestrate child care, provide for us when I had to completely stop working my last semester and then let me not pass. No shame was allowed here. The day of the test was ironic to me. It was the graduate luncheon that everyone could attend and right after was when those of us who needed to test would go to the testing area.

Can you imagine the pressure some may have felt? I didn't, we prayed and fasted until the time of the luncheon. We took our pictures with one another and the instructors, it was our last time together until graduation which was a little over a month away. My prayer partner walked me to the testing classroom. Other classmates came down to encourage us also. The instructors were still being supportive and told us to relax. I was not about to do anything on my own. I asked God where I should sit, which one of these computers is not going to glitch or malfunction in any way. The test was composed of 150 questions. The instructors all sat in front of the class and frequently stood up. They could also see your test progress as far as the question you were on. I got to the 150th questions and had my cursor on it and everything. Then I stopped, sat there, and waited some more. I saw them looking at me. No problem, I had plenty of time available.

Eventually, one of the instructors came over to me and said, "Tanisha, I see you are on your last question, are you done? Is that your choice?" I said "yes." She said, "Well click the button." I told her, "I cannot." She said, "Click the button." I closed my eyes and clicked the button. She said "Congratulations." I knew I had finally passed this annoyance. I opened my eyes that were getting ready to flood with tears. She quickly assisted me from the testing computer while she did whatever she was supposed to. The other instructors stood up and hugged me and then I left the room. I felt as though a weight had been lifted. I called my prayer partner to tell her the news. She said she was sitting in her car and was waiting for all of us. I sat in her vehicle with her, rejoicing and waiting patiently for the others. My God, it was like a force was holding that test. The questions were equally hard with random materials, yet the outcome was different. To God be the Glory!

> *You can't know where you're going until you know where you've been.*
>
> —Maya Angelou

The NCLEX exam is a CAT (Computerized Adaptive Testing), literally, the computer adjusts the difficulty of the question based on the previous answer, consisting of 75- 265 maximum possible questions. You already know, fasting and praying were on deck. I continued with my classmates and prayer partner, of course. Neither of us shared the actual testing date information. The current nurses had enough scary stuff to deal with. Everyone warned, "Oh you shouldn't tell anyone the date it just puts too much pressure on you, and don't give results until you know for sure." Whatever they had going on I didn't care to find out. My concern was how soon can I take my boards and pass? All the while I was praying God would allow me to pass my boards the first time around with the least amount of questions it takes for me to pass.

I had a different study buddy. I was studying with my friend who was also the class valedictorian. We gave it a high-intense two-week run of practicing 150 test questions a day. I didn't put any of the filters on, letting the exam tests bank drop them for me. I completed the questions early in the morning which took about two to two and a half hours. I let it grade the exam, saw the score and logged off to do something, or go somewhere and return hours later towards the night. I knew if I could remember it in my dreams then I knew the material. Then later on in the evening, I would return to the test and review answers that included the incorrect responses and also read the rationale for everything.

That was enough studying for the day and that would equate to six hours of studying a day.

> *Now faith is the substance of things hoped for, the evidence of things not seen.*
> *—Hebrews 11:1 KJV*

There is a waiting period before you can schedule to sit for the boards. We watched daily, checked our email, and logged-in and out often to see if we could register with Pearson Vue. The moment my authorization window opened I was looking to take my exam as soon as possible. According to the instructors and their statistics the longer you wait the less your chances are of success. I did not want to become a statistic. The earliest date was May 5th and it was at a different testing center than my previous boards. I took it but I kept saying this date is too far for me. Here I was done with my classes since March, graduation is the end of April and my boards are scheduled for May. Really wasn't thrilled about this. I brought my concerns to God in prayer. I will never forget the answer I received.

It was Sunday, April 17th, really easy to remember because it is my dad's birthday. I was at church sitting in the middle section towards the front when the church was engaging in intense prayers and the Pastor stopped and said, "Whatever you are believing God for, get that thing on your mind right now. You may think it is impossible but for God it is not. Get that thing on your mind right now and we are going to pray about it." Of course, I let God know specifically that the test date of May 5th was too far and I wanted a closer date. We prayed and said, "Let God Arise!" I went home and logged back onto the Pearson Vue testing site and searched for a new date. Right before my eyes was the very next day Monday, April 18th with a testing time in the morning like I prefer. I got up and walked away from the screen. As I was standing in the kitchen,

I clearly heard the Holy Spirit ask, "Do you want it or not, it is yours for the taking." I said, "I want it!" I returned and clicked on the schedule which automatically canceled the May 5th. Please note that you cannot cancel a test date less than 24 hours, so there was absolutely no turning back from this date. I didn't tell anyone about either of my dates. I prepared my kids for school as usual. I was now getting myself together. What should I wear, I thought? I had the perfect tee-shirt, "Let God Arise" was written across the front. I wore that shirt, didn't comb my hair, sprinkled some water in it, and kept it moving. I had gone to the testing site before just to see how to get there, what the traffic was like, find the exact office, locate the bathroom, and most of all to pray all over the grounds of that place. From the parking lot forward.

When I arrived, I prayed about my parking space before putting my phone in the glove compartment and heading to the site over 30 minutes early. They acknowledged me and told me to be patient while they admitted the appointments for that time. Before I knew it, he was back. I didn't expect it to be my turn so soon. I put my keys in the locker and used the bathroom again. I was not getting up, no matter what. I had trained myself to sit still for a couple of hours. The first gentlemen took my picture. He then led me through a door where there was another gentleman who could see into the testing room. The second gentleman verified who I was again. He asked, "Are you ready?" I said "yes." He said, "Let God Arise." Forgetting about what I was wearing, I said "huh?" He pointed to my shirt then I said, "Yes, Let God Arise."

As we were walking in the test room I prayed and asked God to give me the seat that HE wanted me to have, I also had a seat in my mind. The testing gentleman took me right to the corner. I sat down; my picture popped in the corner of the screen. He gave me all the instructions about my scrap piece of paper and how to get more or get their attention. When he left, I arranged my paper, pencil and I prayed, took a deep breath, and started my exam. Question number one, what is this? Question number two, the same. I kept getting "select all that apply" questions. While I had rigorously studied "select all that apply" I certainly did not want to endure so many of them. These question types are exhaustive and exhausting. About halfway into the test I became annoyed and spoke to God. "God, I know maternal-child/mother-baby. I want mother-baby questions." By now I felt a spirit of authority come up inside of me and I lay my hand on the computer screen and said, In the

Name of Jesus! The very next question "flipped" my screen into mother-baby questions. Yeah! I am smiling and thanking God. The questions were unique, and I didn't recognize them because they were randomly selected and adaptive, but I knew mother-baby without any doubt.

During the time of the HESI blockade, I had laser-focused on mother-baby and "select all that apply" questions. I did not listen to all the noises of the students and multiple testing strategists; I listened to my teacher and chose two test experts and they always emphasized mother-baby and "select all that apply" questions. From my experience, it must be the complexity of mother-baby questions itself. You are ultimately caring for two unique individuals on different ends of the age spectrum. Then "select all that apply" tells what you know or not. I was gleefully at peace with my exam as it progressed until an abrupt stop. I froze when my screen shut off at 80 questions. I sat there and sat there with all the possibilities flooding in. Did you accidentally hit the exam to stop? Did you pass your exam? What's happening?

The examiner came into the room and said you are finished. I looked up at him and asked, "I'm finished?" I was thinking what does that mean? We were instructed not to ask them if they knew the results or anything of that sort. He accompanied me to the one that read my shirt. He said to him, she is finished. He gave me back my identification. I just looked at them both. The other one said, "Have a nice day." I wanted to know what he meant by, "Have a nice day?" I took my key out of the locker and went to the bathroom. I prayed and gave thanks.

Once I was in my car, I retrieved my cell phone from the glove compartment and turned it on. It was then I realized I had completed my exam in about an hour and way ahead of my scheduled time. I thanked God again and started to head on about my day. My brother called me as usual. I spent a little time at the mall since it was a sunny day. My prayer partner called me and asked me what I was up to. I didn't tell her right away. I told her about my trip to the mall then said, "Oh yeah I took my boards this morning." She was surprised. I went over to her house and just relaxed a bit. Nothing much to discuss because she hadn't taken her boards yet. She saw the shirt that I had on. Physically taking the board doesn't make it over, it leads to another part of the process. Should I play the game of log-on, log-off or not, of course. I tried to register for the test again and it wouldn't permit me to do so.

Again, this is one of those, who knows who came up with this, that if you try to register for the exam again and it doesn't let you in then you must have passed the boards. No evidence that I know of supports this but what was going to happen if I tried it out. I couldn't register, okay I will give it a try but I am not one to antagonize myself with the repetition of this act. The results are available in three days if you pay a nominal fee. I had decided that I would not and wait for them to send the results. I could also check the Board of Nursing website for licensure status.

It was Thursday morning of the same week. I received a phone call from another classmate. She wanted me to be the first person she shared her news with. She said she had taken her boards on Tuesday of the same week and her results were in, she PASSED. I congratulated her, yet, still didn't say anything. Until she asked, when are you going to take your boards? I said, I already did, this Monday. She then said your results have got to be in. I said probably since you took yours after me and you have PASSED. She said, let's check and I was like, "Girl, no. I will wait for them to send it or check the boards." She said, "Nope, we are not doing that. We need to know today. Let me check." So, I gave her my access information on the condition that if I did not pass, she should not call back until much later, but if I did pass, she should call me right back. She said she was calling right back because we know you PASSED already.

It was as if time stood still. She called me back and I could see clearly where I was standing in the dining room. The kids had already left for school before she called me to share her good news. She said, in her usual, sweet voice. She stated in just an even tone. "I have to tell you that you PASSED." "Ohhhhhhhhhhhhhh, thank you Jesus! Thank you Jesus! Ohhhhhhhhhh." My goodness, we were laughing and just thanking God. We congratulated each other. She said she needed to go tell her family now because I was the first person she called. The phone could not have hit the dining room table any faster. My feet started running. I took off running up and down the excessively long hallway we had. Our apartment was huge, half of the entire floor. So you can imagine how much running room I had. I was running, shouting, crying, and praising God all at the same time. My God! You did that! Let God Arise and let His enemies be scattered. I just kept saying that. Typing it now, I can feel the power of God that filled me that day. I remember kneeling at the side of my bed, with my hands lifted up thanking Him for how he had marvelously come through not only for me but my family. It was also at that time that I gave my license back to Him. I covered it in the Blood of Jesus.

I called my mom as usual. Moms are such beautiful people. I said, "Mom, what's my name?" She said "Tanisha." I said, "No mom. What's my name?" She said, "Tanisha Hamilton," as soon as she said that I said, "RN!" She said, "Tanisha Hamilton, RN." I said, "Tanisha Hamilton, RN." She started screaming and thanking God and congratulating me. Ohhhhhhh my! Jesus! When He does it, there is no denying. Years later I am penning this testimony and I still get overwhelmed with His love. I notified my instructor, the one who was there physically until the very end. She was there at my last chance at HESI. She came over to my computer asking me if I was done. She encouraged me to hit the button. It was so powerful. Yes, I was heart-broken and distraught during the failed times of HESI, but I kept telling her God is able. I trust Him. Then I sent a text to my clinical instructor to tell him and he called back. That was enough for the school to be notified. I received a lot of phone calls.

Interestingly, I spoke to the same people daily for years in what looks like the same order they called. I gave my prayer partner the news and it was mass hysteria again. I was going to see and celebrate with her shortly. I logged onto the Boards of Nursing website, searched myself by name in one field, and I saw my license number. I logged out and searched on the testing site also. I took pictures of every screen, just to make sure that it didn't disappear. I had evidence of what I saw. Continuing to celebrate with my friends, I sent a picture of my name on the Board website, this was non-debatable. My opener stated, "Look what the Lord has done." I received a special call from a fellow RN, a few moments into being licensed 'I can say that, Jesus!' She was so excited for me. She said she was in the breakroom and she showed it to them at work.

I began with this group of amazing healthcare professions starting from when I was a certified nursing assistant and nurse extern. Please don't despise small beginnings. Small is not a state of being less than, it just means it is the process to a greater future. I could not wait for my kids to get home to share our good news. We went out to dinner to celebrate! This was the night that I actually rested.

A goal is a dream with a finish line.
—Duke Ellington

The wait is over. I am a registered nurse weeks before the graduation ceremony. I was not alone at this juncture, some of my fellow classmates took the plunge early and were now officially my RN colleagues. It was electrifying. I didn't know that during commencement those who had already passed their boards would be recognized and asked to stand. They then asked other nurses in the concessions to stand. I was still smiling. My family, friends, and even our primary care provider attended graduation on my behalf. I really wanted this behind me so that I could enjoy my parents visiting for a long time and celebrate my son's birthday without having to study. Apparently, my kids told my mom that I was crazy in nursing school. Go figure!

Double Weekends

I will not take 'but' for an answer.
—Langston Hughes

I took almost a month off, intentionally, and non-intentionally at the same time. I mean I am a registered nurse now; you should start looking for a job. So, I did, but I also slept. I was so sleep-deprived. I would get calls about going out to celebrate. What are you doing? I am sleeping. That's what I wanted to do to celebrate. NCLEX was defeated, graduation was exhilarating, my son enjoyed his birthday, we celebrated my birthday in the midst also and my parents' visit was greatly appreciated. All of these had come to a pleasant end and I wanted to sleep.

My parents had financed my last semester of nursing school and for a moment after. I searched for hospitals in the area and found the one that was hiring new graduates and had good compensation. I called, spoke with a knowledgeable receptionist. The Human Resources personnel at this particular hospital told me that I could complete the application that day and it would be forwarded to the manager.

God did it again, I met with the manager the same day, he offered me the position and I told him that I had three other friends. Two of us for dayshift and two for the night shift. God did not just do it for me, He did it for my friends as well. I had spent so much time with them I knew the schedule that would work for them.

It's funny the manager said you came to get yourself a position but you are getting your three friends an opportunity too, I like that. Tell them to fill out the application today so I can get the interviews arranged. I called my friends one-by-one and told them I got you a job here is the information and I told him what time you would be calling. This story needs to be shared. I called one of them and said, hey are you looking for a job. She said no, not yet. I am just enjoying being on vacation. I will start looking next week. I said, uh, no. Your vacation is over. I got you a position. You must fill out the application today. I already told the manager about you, your kids, and the schedule. I even told him a pay rate; she didn't have experience working in the medical field so I didn't want her to accept less than she should have. She said ok. She called the facility, interviewed that day and the rest is history. We worked together until I went into a travel nursing opportunity. Too funny. Where do I get off telling someone, their vacation is over?

Whenever I start a job, I am already identifying my exit date, this is a habit. I have no negative basis or experience, but from day one or within the week I know when I am leaving. This forces me to take advantage of the opportunities they present, may it be training, seminars, etc. I look at a calendar and I write a resignation letter.

It always has the same parts: thanks for the opportunity to work with a supportive team, I have learned a lot, I have grown my skills and I will be furthering my educational and professional opportunities. It is true in the end.

CHAPTER 9
CUT THE UMBILICAL CORD

While I was still in school, I had a peaked interest in travel nursing. Being able to travel and provide for my children while being part of a great profession was a beautiful thing to me. During school, we reviewed different specialties. The one thing I almost forgot to mention was once I was a licensed registered nurse, I called different travel nurse companies to find out what their specific requirements and which specialties were best to travel with regarding compensation and opportunities. The common statement was a minimum of two years' experience. You should stick to critical care nursing such as intensive care unit, cardiac/telemetry, progressive care, neonatal intensive care unit, emergency room, and labor & delivery.

Once I started working my full-time position as a medical-surgical nurse. I needed to add another specialty. I got an additional position on a neurological/stroke-telemetry unit. I was very honest with the second position in that I would fulfill my scheduled requirements, but I needed to make my schedule because my first position took scheduling priority. That was a mutual agreement. God was favoring this new RN. I was maximizing my skills sets. I also had my Basic Life Support (BLS), Advanced Cardiac Life Support (ACLS), and National Institute of Health Stroke Scale (NIHSS) certifications. As soon as I was approaching my year mark, I started to renew communication with the travel companies again. The door was about to be taken off of the hinges for me. I was fortunate to obtain a diligent recruiter. He told me what I had researched, the usual standard was two years.

That's cool for others, but I know a God who does the impossible and will always grant me favor. He submitted me for a travel assignment to North Carolina. The manager was interested in interviewing me because of my intense specialties regardless of the timeframe. She offered me the position and stated that she would communicate that to the recruiters, and they would get back with me shortly. Shortly was more like secondly or minutely. This position at that time to me had a very intimidating feature on two hands. One, I had to pass the rhythm interpretation strip. There was no room for error. There was no do-over or second chance. The second, I brought my children with me. I agreed to allow the travel nursing company to find my place of residence; learned my lesson in this area and many other travel nurse areas.

I can share at another juncture may it be a conversation or book of practical tips that will ensure a successful experience and a continued desire to be a travel nurse. Here's what I have mastered as a travel nurse.

The travel company would provide me with a hotel for four days because during this time the hospital had an all or none exam. You either pass the test and start your assignment or fail the test and your contract is terminated immediately. As a newbie, I had never heard of this. The exam was on cardiac rhythm strips. Sure, I knew how to interrupt strips and I was ACLS certified, but what were they coming with, the unknown can be gripping if you allow it. All travelers would arrive at the Human Resources office bright and early Tuesday morning, get our badges, receive a tour, do standard onboarding, and then take the test. I have learned to not sit in the room with people too early prior to the start of your exam because the chatter amongst them can make you doubt your skills, I mean seasoned cardiac nurses were not passing the strip interpretation review sessions.

When I got back to my hotel, I called my pastor from Texas at that time and communicated the seriousness of this test. If you don't pass the exam, your assignment is over. That would not have been too bad if I hadn't had my children with me. Remember, I wanted to travel and have the opportunity to provide but allow my kids to experience different places. I only worked three days a week, that's one of the beauties of travel nursing as I have come to find out. Again, more about that later in another book. He prayed and then I continued to study. I wasn't going to rack my brains because I studied and believed. The moment of truth. The exam was computerized. The rhythms were like none I had seen but I knew the concepts of determining the rhythm. Follow the steps every time and you enhance your chance of excelling.

There was a strip I was not sure of other than a bad day for the person with that rhythm. I called the instructor over to me and I explained to her what I saw and why I thought that the answer was the one I had highlighted. She didn't agree or disagree, she just asked, "Is that what you think the answer is based on what you said?" I said, yes. At that moment I remembered my HESI test, in which I had the cursor on the last question and the instructor asked are you done, if you are, go ahead and hit the button.

Woohoo, the exam was over, but my assignment wasn't over. I passed the test. She gave us all a much-needed break. I sprung a leak like a water fountain, a nervous pee. I called my pastor and told him the good news. He congratulated me and said the church members would be checking on us, which they faithfully did. I couldn't wait for the day to be over to get to my greatest supporters, my children, and let them know we were leaving the hotel and going to our duplex tomorrow. The relief was sure. New assignment, time to explore this quaint place. Day one of a two-day orientation. Yeah, short and direct is how that goes.

This assignment was a telemetry assignment they said, yet, they neglected to say that it was a trache-vented, telemetry, dialysis unit. All of the patients had a trache-vent combination with other comorbidities. Every nurse has something in patient care that they are willing to negotiate care with another nurse to do for them. Lo' and behold mine was trache care. My secretions would start working overtime. I chewed so much gum that summer that was the only thing that counteracted my salivary surplus. Now, cool, I will assist a fellow nurse mate with that care. I was thrown into the trenches of facing that task.

What a welcome, the first day they also had the Employee Appreciation Week Celebration. The food was delicious, they had Moon Pies, if you don't know you better ask somebody. Now this is how you welcome someone, party time, great food, the employees were friendly, even took character pictures with people I just met but we recognized each other from orientation or the same unit. I really enjoyed working with the majority of the people. Until I was introduced to the patient care assignment treatment of the travel nurse I had heard about. Why was the census four and I kept getting five or six? I know it's not always going to be an even number of patients, but surely it couldn't be my turn especially if others had fewer patients, and didn't work the previous day like I did. I noticed but I didn't say anything until the monitor technicians who worked every day said I seem like I have given you so many strips each day. I said, it sure seems like that. I gathered my evidence, which was keeping my patient assignment sheets in the hospital because I definitely didn't want anyone's personal information with me outside of work. It was the same charge nurse. So this was not what we were going to do for thirteen weeks, the length of my contract, which I had already decided I wasn't going to extend.

Remember, the exit strategy comes pretty early. I have learned so many skills, strategies, and implementations of travel nursing that I have shared with other nurses I have met on assignments. They take my number and seek my advice from the beginning to the end of each transaction. I didn't know my experience would prove to be so insightful, purposeful, and valuable to other nurses wanting to transition.

CHAPTER 10
THE 3 Y'S MEN

Let me introduce you to the 3 Y's Men. People ask me how I made it through nursing school as a single mother with two school-aged children. I would often answer in summary with the 3 Y's men. But now I have left you wondering, right? So let me introduce the 3 Y's men to you. In this corner, we have the infamous Cr (Y) er. I often drenched my pillows with hot tears. If you do not know what hot tears are let me explain. Hot tears come from the depths of your being from agony and toiling. An intense yearning to apprehend what is for you. You are in active pursuit, but the goal line seems to push further back at times. Hot tears are the most inexpressible tears that I have ever known. My voice left; my words could not effectively articulate what I needed.

In the other corner, we have the Pra (Y) er. This one you will need to learn or become more intense in fervor and accuracy. I read books on warfare prayers. I needed divine intervention on the highest level. I remember watching a movie called, War Room. That was my example. I cleared everything in my master closet out and went into intense prayer. This coupled with having a prayer partner is invaluable in obtaining victory.

Last but certainly not least, is Stud(Y) a lot. This has got to be an understatement. You must study. There is not any way around it. I would take my books in the bathroom. Review recorded class discussions while cooking, make note cards for the dentist and doctor's office, or any place that I was going to be stationary for a while. Then, when my family would oblige me. I would teach my kids. Then if they did not want to listen, you guessed it, I could teach it to an empty room. I wrote on my whiteboard and all. Please do not negate the 3Y's men. Awkwardly enough, they did not come in any certain order and sometimes they came at the same time.

I prayed a lot. I studied a lot and I cried a lot. This begs repeating, they came in no certain order, and sometimes they came at the same time. If you please allow me to leave with you the most valuable truths that I have experienced and penned to serve for your inspiration is to wholeheartedly listen to God, consult with Him to make decisions. He will provide Clear Executive Orders for your life. I pushed. God Pushed. We Pushed…and so can you too boldly and strategically lay hold of what God has in store for you. I'M YOUR PUSHER!

www.ingramcontent.com/pod-product-compliance
Lightning Source LLC
LaVergne TN
LVHW051154080426
835508LV00021B/2615